Y

YOU CHOOSE BOOKS

The WINCHESTER Mystery House

A CHILLING INTERACTIVE ADVENTURE

by Matt Doeden

CAPSTONE PRESS
a capstone imprint

You Choose Books are published by Capstone Press,
1710 Roe Crest Drive, North Mankato, Minnesota 56003
www.mycapstone.com

Library of Congress Cataloging-in-Publication Data
Cataloging-in-publication information is on file with the Library of Congress.
ISBN 978-1-5157-2577-0 (library binding)
ISBN 978-1-5157-2581-7 (ebook PDF)

Editorial Credits
Anthony Wacholtz, editor; Heidi Thompson, designer; Wanda Winch, media researcher;
Laura Manthe, production specialist

Photo Credits
AwesomeShot Studios: Oren Arieli, cover (all), 4-36, 45-104; ©Winchester Mystery
House, San Jose, CA, 39, 42; Shutterstock: happykanppy, old paper painting design,
Plateresca, grunge label design, run4it, grunge ink painting design, saki80, grunge
frame design

Printed in Canada.
009633F16

Table of Contents

INTRODUCTION

YOU are about to enter the Winchester Mystery House. The massive maze-like home was built over nearly four decades with one sole purpose—to ward off evil spirits. And now you're inside. What will you find? Will you try to escape or delve deeper into the mansion? Will you uncover the mysteries of this haunted house? And if you do, will you make it out alive?

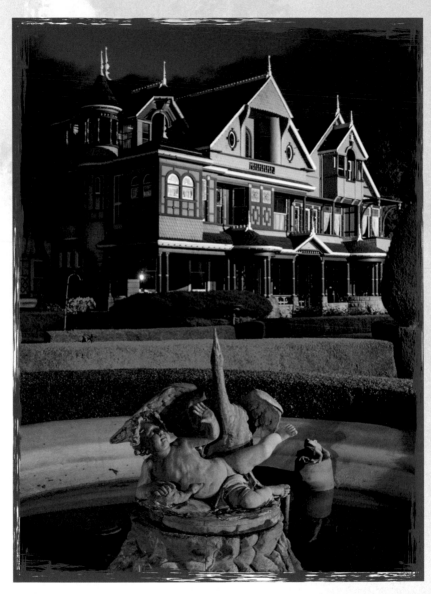

Shrubs, fountains, and statues decorate the gardens of the Winchester Mystery House.

THE WINCHESTER MYSTERY HOUSE

"Hey, Amir, thanks again for helping me get this job. I can't believe I actually get to work here. I've read all about this place."

Amir flashes you a grin. "No problem."

Amir's dad owns a landscaping company. When Amir told you the company had landed a job in the gardens of the famous Winchester Mystery House, you knew that you wanted in. You've always been fascinated by the paranormal.

"I never knew you were so excited about gardening," Amir says. "We get a job at a haunted house and suddenly you can't wait to start pulling weeds. Now pay attention to what you're doing. Those rose bushes are more than a hundred years old. Watch out for the ..."

Turn the page.

"Ouch!" you shout as something sharp cuts at your finger.

"... thorns," finishes Amir.

Between the afternoon heat of the California sun and the sight of your own blood beading up on your finger, you start to feel a bit dizzy.

The white door seen on the second story of the Winchester Mystery House is the infamous Door to Nowhere.

"Whoa, you're looking a little pale there,"
Amir says, coming to your side and grabbing you
by the arm. You feel your knees buckling, and
darkness creeps in at the edges of your vision.
Amir helps you to the ground, fanning you with
his work gloves.

"You look like you're going to faint," Amir
says. "I think you need to cool off."

Amir glances over his shoulder. His father has
taken the company van to check on another job.
There's nowhere for you to get out of the heat,
except inside the house.

"Guess we don't have anywhere else to go,"
Amir says, gesturing.

"We're not supposed to go inside, remember?"
you argue. The instructions were quite clear. The
house is off limits.

Turn the page.

Amir shakes his head and shrugs his shoulders. "I don't think it'll be a problem," he says. "The house is closed today. No tours. Nobody will care if we go in to cool off for a few minutes."

Amir helps you to your feet and leads you in through a set of doors. The cool air and shade are an instant relief. Your lightheadedness is already going away.

"Let's find someplace where we can wash out that scrape," Amir says.

The two of you head down a hallway. Only this is no ordinary hallway. It twists and turns for no apparent reason. You pass a strange stairway with tiny steps and a wall full of stained-glass windows designed to look like spider webs. It's fascinating. As the two of you explore deeper, you realize that your scrape isn't even bothering you anymore.

stained glass windows with spider web designs

"You know, there are supposed to be miles of passageways in this place," you tell Amir. "Some people think that all of the rooms haven't even been found yet. Think about it—rooms that nobody has seen in nearly a hundred years!"

Turn the page.

"Yeah," Amir replies. "And Dad says that the lady who had it built did it all to ward off evil spirits. She thought that turning her house into a maze would keep them from following her."

The two of you laugh. But as the laughter dies down, you can't help but feel a chill at the thought. The room feels instantly cold, as though you're standing directly under a vent. You look to Amir. He's shivering as well.

That's when you hear the footsteps behind you.

To run away from the footsteps, go to page 13.

To move toward the footsteps, turn to page 16.

To look for somewhere to hide, turn to page 32.

The footsteps are faint, but it sounds like they're approaching. You and Amir look at each other, eyes wide. "Run!" you whisper. You're not sure why, but you feel a very sudden, very desperate urge to get away.

Together you bound down the twisting hallway, almost crashing into the walls as you weave and duck through the maze-like corridors. Finally, after countless turns, you both fall to the floor in a heap, gasping for breath. You listen for several silent moments. No footsteps. Nothing but the distant tick-tick-ticking of an unseen clock. The panic and dread you felt seem to melt away.

Now it all seems ridiculous. You can tell by the look on Amir's face that he feels the same. You both start to laugh.

"Let's get out of here," Amir says.

Turn the page.

The narrow switchback staircase in the Winchester Mystery House zigzags back and forth.

But there's a problem. In your panic, you didn't pay much attention to where you were going. And now … "I think we're lost," you say with a groan.

"Shh!" Amir whispers, waving a hand at you. "Do you hear that?"

You start to shake your head when … there! You do hear it. It's a series of low, droning notes, a low, mournful melody. Music!

"It's organ music," you whisper back. There's no mistaking it now. It's distant, more an echo than a song. But it is definitely organ music. And it's coming from deeper inside the house.

To follow the music, turn to page 20.

To head back in the direction of the footsteps, turn to page 23.

"Hey!" you shout. The word echoes through the empty hallway. "Is somebody there? Hello?"

No answer. "Come on," you say, half-dragging Amir back in the direction of the footsteps. But as you move back through the hallway, you pause.

"No, it's coming from that way," Amir says, pointing down another hallway. You're not so sure. You stand there, staring down both corridors. At one moment, the footsteps seem to be coming from the corridor that veers right. The next moment, they seem to be coming from your left. And occasionally, it almost sounds as if they're behind you.

"It's this way!" Amir seems more certain than you are, so you follow his lead. The corridor, lined with lacquered wood panels, takes you deeper and deeper into the house.

The Winchester Mystery House is filled with long hallways and abnormal structures.

But just as you seem to be closing in on the source of the sound, the footsteps seem to be coming from another direction. Then another. And another.

"What's going on here?" Amir asks.

Turn the page.

You're not sure you want to know the answer. You look behind you, considering that it might be time to try retracing your steps. But before you can suggest it, a loud slam shakes the house. The lights flicker. A cold draft rolls across your skin.

Amir screams and runs. You whirl about, ready to chase after your friend. But as you turn, a chill runs down your spine and you freeze in your tracks.

You're not alone. And it's not Amir. You can hear his thundering footsteps retreating down the hallway. There, not more than 20 feet from you, stands a figure. It's the shape of an old woman, draped in long, flowing robes. She's all white and transparent. Your heart races, and your knees buckle. The apparition stares straight at you, eyes black as coal. She opens her mouth, as if to speak. All you hear is a low whisper, almost beyond your threshold of hearing. You can't make it out.

Slowly, the apparition turns. She raises her hand, index finger extended, and beckons you. Her message is impossible to mistake. She wants you to follow her.

To follow the ghost, turn to page 26.

To bolt past her and try to find Amir, turn to page 55.

"That doesn't make any sense," Amir insists. "The house is supposed to be empty today. This place is starting to creep me out."

You elbow him in the ribs. "A little adventure for us, nothing wrong with that. Let's see what this is all about."

Together you creep through the dimly lit hallways. You try to keep track of your movements—down this corridor, up this strange staircase with the tiny steps, past that locked room. But it doesn't take long before you're completely turned around.

"Are we lost?" Amir groans. He's starting to get worried. You continue to follow the sound of the music, though it never really feels like you're getting any closer. Under other circumstances, you'd love to take the time to check out each and every room. But this isn't a tour, and you just want to get back outside.

You come into a room lined with fireplaces. "The Hall of Fires," you whisper. You've read about this place. The room's large windows reveal near darkness outside.

"How long have we been in here?" Amir asks, puzzled.

Tourists have said the Hall of Fires was frigid, even during the summer months.

Turn the page.

Before you can answer, you feel a sudden chill. Then, with a *whooosh*, all of the fireplaces burst to life. The door behind you slams shut. Amir screams. Flames crackle all around you, spreading dancing patterns of light and shadow on the walls. And yet … the room still feels cold.

Amir rushes back to the closed door, but it won't budge. "Locked!" he says, terror creeping into his voice.

One door stands open. You can't help but feel that it's an invitation. But … to what?

To proceed through the open door, turn to page 38.

To try to break down the door behind you and flee, turn to page 53.

Something about this feels wrong. Sinister. Suddenly, you don't feel much like adventure.

"Let's get out of here," you say.

"You don't have to ask me twice," Amir answers. You can tell he's getting spooked. The two of you turn around and start retracing your steps. But that proves harder than you imagine. The twists and turns have you completely disoriented.

"None of this is familiar," you say with a sigh.

Amir shakes his head. "Great. We're lost."

You pass by what appears to be a reading room. A warm light glows inside. You stop for a closer look. An ornate chair sits next to a lantern. A small flame flickers in the lantern, its light bathing the room in warm, orange colors.

Turn the page.

"Weeeeelcome." The whisper freezes both of you in your tracks. Without warning, books start to fly off the bookshelves.

With a scream, you turn and run. You sprint down the hallways, nearly wiping out as you round the corners. You run until you realize Amir is no longer with you.

"Amir!" you shout. "Amir, where are you?" You move through the enormous mansion, shouting out for your friend. At one point, you can hear him shouting back. But it all sounds very distant. Panic is setting in. What was that voice? And where is your friend?

You race through the hallways, desperate to find Amir. Purely by accident, you stumble across the exit back out to the gardens. For a split second, you feel a wave of relief, until you realize that Amir's still inside.

Look closely at the mirror—the stairway runs right into the ceiling!

Your hand rests on the door. You could leave right now. You could call for help. But that will take time. And Amir is inside with … whatever that was. Can you leave your friend? You close your eyes and take a deep breath.

To go back inside to search for Amir, turn to page 29.

To leave the house now, turn to page 51.

In this maze of a house, you're never going to find Amir. You watch as the white figure moves slowly away from you. Something about the way she moves, hovering just above the floor, gives you the chills, but she doesn't seem threatening. An invitation from a ghost—that's an offer you're not likely to ever get again in your life. With a deep breath, you decide to take it.

one of the many upstairs corridors

You follow, still wary, staying back a dozen paces or so, as she leads you deeper and deeper into the house. The ghost moves slowly but at a steady pace. She seems to pay no attention to you. You wonder if you should simply turn around and go the other way. But your curiosity won't let you do that. You have to know where this is leading.

Finally, the ghost leads you out a pair of double doors, into an enclosed courtyard. Then, abruptly, the ghost stops. Behind her stands a small bell tower. She slowly nods her head toward the tower. The message is clear: She wants you to go up.

There's one small problem. There's no staircase. The only way you can see to get to the bell tower is by climbing a rickety-looking ladder to a nearby roof, then stepping across to the tower. You look up, then back at the ghost, just in time to see her fade from sight.

Turn the page.

Some visitors have claimed to hear the bell ring 13 times.

The ladder stands there, waiting. "This is crazy," you whisper to yourself.

To start climbing, turn to page 45.

To turn around and leave the courtyard, turn to page 48.

You close your eyes and sigh. The way out is right here, but you can't leave. You've got to find your friend.

"I'm coming, Amir!" you shout, charging back into the twisted hallways. As night creeps in, the hallways are darker. Every corner feels more sinister. Every now and then, you hear Amir's voice, distant and muffled. But getting to him is maddening. Nothing in this house goes the way you'd expect. You start up a staircase, only to find that it runs straight into the ceiling! The hallways zig and zag, sending you down dead ends and making you feel like you're going in circles. Just when you think you're making progress, you find that you've gone in a circle.

"Help! Help!" It's Amir's voice, and this time it's close. You charge toward the sound, finally finding him clinging to a doorway. The room beyond is dimly lit, and he's staring inside.

Turn the page.

"Amir," you say.

"Shhhh." He doesn't even turn. "There is something here."

Anxiously, you peer inside. The room is bathed in soft candlelight from an ornate, old-fashioned chandelier overhead. You notice that one of the candles remains unlit.

In the far corner stands a strange figure. It seems to fade in and out, but at times, the image is clear. It's an old woman. She's staring up at the chandelier. Her face appears distraught.

Slowly, she lowers her gaze until it's fixed upon you. She raises a thin, almost skeletal arm and points a bony finger. You look up again at the chandelier. Twelve candles are lit. She seems to be pointing at the unlit candle.

"Heeeeelp." The sound is more a gust of wind than a spoken word. Is she asking you to light the candle?

"Let's get out of here," Amir says, tugging on your shirt. But you can't take your eyes off of the ghost before you.

"Come on!" Amir tugs harder. You can hear growing panic in his voice.

To go with Amir, turn to page 84.

To try to light the remaining candle, turn to page 87.

You and Amir turn toward each other, jaws dropped.

"Hide!" you whisper. As quickly and quietly as you can, you hurry to the closest door. You turn the knob and slip inside.

Instantly, you feel as though you've stepped into a cold spot. It's like this room is 20 degrees colder than the hallway. And you're overcome by a powerful sense that you're being watched. The hairs on the back of your neck stand up. You keep looking over your shoulder, convinced that something is lurking behind you. But nothing is there.

"It's the Blue Room—the séance room," Amir whispers. "I read about this place. This is where Sarah Winchester spoke to the dead. This is where she asked them for guidance on how to build this place."

Tourists who have visited the séance room have reported temperature changes and feelings of dizziness and nausea.

"Okay," you whisper, slowly backing toward the door. "This is beyond creepy. Let's get out of ..."

SLAM! Each of the room's four doors slam shut at once. You and Amir run to each of the doors and pull on the knobs frantically, but none of them will budge—the only one you can open appears to be a closet. Amir steps back and launches his entire body into one of the doors. But he just slams into it with a dull thud and falls to the floor, groaning.

Turn the page.

You're trapped.

The lights flicker and dim. A cold gust of air swirls around the room. You look on in shock and terror as a strange glowing light floats in the corner of the room. It descends down onto your friend.

Amir's hands shake. His head jerks and his eyes roll back into his head. His entire face twists and contorts, until it barely even looks like Amir anymore. Then, as suddenly as they began, the strange movements stop.

With a ghostly calm, Amir turns and stares at you. But you have no doubt. Whoever is staring at you though those eyes, it's not Amir.

Behind your friend's body, behind whatever it is that has taken control of it, one of the room's doors slowly opens. Its hinges whine with the sound of metal scraping metal.

To talk to Amir, turn to page 36.

To run, turn to page 81.

Amir looks pale, his expression empty.

"Hey, Amir," you say, tentatively reaching out a hand. "Bud?"

Amir continues to stare at you ... through you. He opens his mouth and speaks. But the voice is not his. It's a woman's voice, but faded. Almost like a recording.

"Leave this house."

A single rose lies next to a picture of Sarah Winchester in her bedroom. She believed that spirits roamed her house.

"Who are you?" you ask. But you feel like you already know the answer.

"They are coming." The speech is monotone. Each word seems like a struggle. But the voice goes on. "The spirits. Always coming. They will find you. Nowhere to hide. You. Must. Go."

Your heart is racing. Every fiber of your being tells you to run right now. But you're not leaving without Amir.

To grab Amir and drag him out, turn to page 70.

To try to talk the spirit into leaving his body, turn to page 72.

You don't see any other choice. You step through the open door. Behind you, you can hear Amir throwing his body against the closed door, desperately trying to escape.

The hallway beyond the open door is dimly lit. It looks like there might be some sort of flame lantern or lamp ahead. Nothing about it feels real. You can barely feel your feet as you creep through the darkness. It's quiet ... too quiet. And you constantly find yourself rubbing your eyes. Everything looks just a little hazy, a little foggy, like you're seeing the world through smeared eyeglasses.

You come upon a room with an ornate glass lantern hanging in a corner. Its light gives the room a warm, orange glow. The floor is covered in a thin film of sawdust.

In the center of the room, you see the number 1906 drawn in the dust, as if by a finger, yet there's not a footprint to be seen. Uncut lumber litters the floor. You hear the pound-pound-pounding of a hammer.

You turn to Amir, only to realize he's not there. "Amir!" You try to shout the name, but it only comes out as a whisper.

Sarah Winchester employed many workers to build and upkeep her enormous house.

Turn the page.

It's a large room. Near the back, you spot the figures of two men standing over a pair of sawhorses. They don't seem to notice you. As you approach, you realize that you can almost see through them. They're pale, washed out. Ghosts.

You stifle a sneeze, and the ghosts immediately turn in your direction. That's when the ground begins to shake. The walls creak and groan. Wooden beams crash down from the ceiling. The men shout, turn to run. The doorway caves in. Clouds of dust fill the air. From above, you hear an enormous crash. Screaming, certain death is heartbeats away, you bring your arms up, instinctively trying to cover your head.

But then, in an instant, it's over. There's no trace of the two men. That dreamlike haze has lifted. The room seems … older. Yet the burning lantern remains.

There, on the floor, that number remains, etched in dust. 1906. Beyond it, near where the two ghosts had appeared, stands an open door. Through the threshold, you can see a steep, narrow staircase leading down.

Amir rushes in. "There you are!" he says, grabbing you by the arm. "Come on. I managed to unlock the door. We can leave now."

As scared as you are, you're also curious. Are you really ready to leave?

To investigate the staircase, turn to page 42.

To turn around and leave with Amir, turn to page 90.

You point. "1906 ... what is that? What does that mean?"

Amir pauses. "I dunno. A year, maybe? Who cares? Let's get out of here."

He's right. You remember reading about it now. The huge earthquake in 1906—it shook the entire area. Was that what you just saw? Some sort of weird flashback?

The 1906 earthquake damaged several areas of the house. Sarah Winchester thought it was a sign from the spirits that she had spent too much money on the house's construction.

Shaking your head, you take a step toward the open door. It's pitch black inside.

"Hey," Amir says behind you. "Hey! Are you crazy?"

You're so focused on what's in front of you that you barely hear your friend. You grab the lantern and step across the threshold. A steep staircase leads down. The air below smells stale and musty. The stairs creak and complain with every step you take. You're a little worried one might collapse right out from underneath you.

But the stairs don't collapse. As you step down onto a wooden floor below, you shine the lantern's light all around. What you see takes your breath away. It's a wine cellar. The walls are lined with racks, filled with countless wine bottles. You grab one at random. Its label reads "1891."

Turn the page.

Behind you, you can hear Amir's footsteps on the stairs.

"Whoa," he gasps, taking in the scene. "Look at this. My grandpa is a wine collector. Bottles this old must be worth thousands of dollars. Each! Maybe more. Come on, grab all you can carry. We're gonna be rich!"

Something about that doesn't feel right, though. These bottles don't belong to you. You can't just take them, can you? Then again, it's been almost a hundred years. It's not stealing if nobody knows they're here, right?

To carry as many bottles as you can, turn to page 58.

To leave the wine here, turn to page 60.

Here goes nothing, you tell yourself. You start to climb, questioning your own sanity with every step. Up, up, up.

You pull your body onto the rooftop and look down. A bright, full moon illuminates lush gardens below.

a view of the gardens from the third story

Turn the page.

There! What was that? Down in the garden, someone moves through the hedges. Not someone … something. A human shape, transparent, floating rather than walking. As you focus your gaze, you realize the shapes are everywhere. It's as if your eyes are being opened to another world. This house—the entire property—is infested with spirits.

That's when the bell in the tower begins to toll. Ding …. ding … ding …. You count twelve rings.

Twelve. Does that mean midnight? You glance at your watch. It's 2 AM! Is it possible? Have you been in this house that long? That doesn't make any sense. And why 12 rings?

That's it! Sarah Winchester was obsessed with the number 13. Was it her spirit who brought you here to ring the bell one final time? A long rope hangs down before you. Your heart is racing.

You reach up and pull the cord to the bell. It sings out with a deep, resonant BOONNNNG!

A powerful gust of wind rushes over the grounds. You instinctively shield your eyes. By the time you open them again, all of the spirits are gone, as if the ringing of the bell somehow freed them.

Then you notice something else. A police car. You can just see it near the grounds' main parking lot. Its red and blue lights are on. Uh oh. Has someone reported a break-in? Did you trip some silent alarm? Are you in serious trouble now? What should you do?

To hide, turn to page 63.

To try to signal the officer, turn to page 66.

47

"This is crazy," you mutter to yourself. You feel like you're stuck in a dream. What's going on here? Has your imagination run away with you?

Whatever is happening here, you're not going to play along any more. Resolved, you turn around, marching back through the double doors, determined to find your friend and get out of here once and for all.

the main floor staircase

You move through the house, listening for Amir, but you can't hear a thing. No spooky sounds. No sudden chills. Nothing. Just an empty house. It's almost as if all of it was your imagination. The only sounds are your own footsteps and the growling of your stomach. You realize it's been a long time since you've eaten anything.

That's when you smell it. The odor is unmistakable. It's chicken soup.

To continue your search for Amir and an exit, turn to page 50.

To go in search of the soup, turn to page 75.

Why would you be smelling chicken soup? That's impossible. You shake your head, as if trying to clear it. Your imagination is running wild in this crazy house. Imagining that spirits are leading you through the house, that there's some ghostly bowl of soup somewhere. It's crazy. You feel like you're losing your grip on reality. Your hands shake. Your ears ring. You just aren't yourself.

You try to retrace your steps, calling out Amir's name every few seconds. After several minutes, you finally hear a reply. It's not a voice, but a *thump-thump-thumping,* as if someone is beating on the floor or a wall.

To follow the sound, turn to page 78.

To ignore the sound and get out of here, turn to page 92.

You can't do it. You won't. You tell yourself that you're leaving so that you can call for help. But deep down, you know that you're leaving because you're terrified of whatever it was you saw inside the house. You can't bear the thought of facing it again.

The outside of the Winchester Mystery House was created with a Victorian style. It features balconies, turrets, and a castle-like appearance.

Turn the page.

"I'll bring help, Amir. Hang on," you shout back at the house. The word feels somehow empty.

Several hours later, you're sitting in the back of a police car, drinking from a bottle of water.

"Don't worry, kid," says an officer, peering over a notepad. "We'll find your friend. It's just a house. He's in there somewhere. Now let's get you home."

As the car pulls away, you can't take your eyes off the Winchester Mystery House. You can almost swear you hear the low wailing of organ music, even from outside. And you have a dark, dark feeling that you're never going to see Amir again. Can you ever forgive yourself?

THE END

To follow another path, turn to page 12.
To learn more about the Winchester Mystery House,
turn to page 97.

"No chance I'm going that way," you say. You turn and start to kick at the locked door behind you. Amir grabs a small wooden table and manages to bash a hole through the door. Instantly, the fireplaces go dead. The room turns from cold to downright frigid. And it's almost completely dark. You find yourself shivering, goosebumps covering your arms.

Amir doesn't stop. He batters at the door, finally kicking it open. He charges through and sprints down the hallway.

"Wait!" you shout, trying to keep up. But Amir is in a panic. He's not thinking clearly. As you start to slip through the mangled doorway, a sound freezes you in your tracks. It's a voice ... more like the echo of a voice. It's calling out your name.

Turn the page.

Slowly, you turn. The figure standing before you is little more than a mist. You rub your eyes, just to be sure it's really there. Your heart is racing. Your legs feel like jelly.

The figure moves closer. The face is wrapped up in some sort of haze, like looking through a frosted window. Yet you can still make out features—deep, hollow, lifeless eye sockets. A long, drawn face, half covered in flowing, unbrushed hair.

The spirit opens its mouth. Inside, all you can see is pure blackness. And the smell ... death.

A terrible scream echoes through the enormous mansion. It's the last sound you ever hear.

THE END

To follow another path, turn to page 12.
To learn more about the Winchester Mystery House,
turn to page 97.

The fear wells up inside you. Every fiber of your being tells you one thing: RUN!

At first, you're not sure your legs will even carry you. But the fear also gives you a surge of adrenaline. You tear off as fast as you can go—right toward the white figure floating before you. It screams as you try to rush by. A blast of icy wind slams you into the wall, sending you sprawling to the floor.

"Nooooo!" you shout, shuffling backward on all fours as the white shape descends upon you. Its eyes glow deep red, its mouth opens wider and wider. You're helpless to stop it.

The pain doesn't last long. Soon, you feel nothing at all. You sense yourself rising, up ... up. But, with a dull sense of confusion, you realize your body remains on the floor. You try to leave, but you feel somehow tied to this place, as though a giant anchor holds you here.

Turn the page.

One visitor is said to have heard a voice singing in the Venetian dining room. Another guest claimed to have seen a shadow in the dining room that resembled a short woman, even though no women were in the room.

In time, you learn to harness your anger. As people pass through the house, you desperately try to let them know you're there. You slam doors. You make the lights dim and flicker. You even try grabbing people by the arms to get their attention.

No one seems to understand that all you want is help. People scream. They run from you. Nothing you do makes any of them try to talk to you. In fact, the harder you try to get their attention, the more scared they seem to be.

With the increase in strange activity in the house, fewer and fewer visitors come. Then the entire section of the house where you died is boarded up. Dark. Silent. Empty.

You're trapped and alone. Terrified. You don't know how to leave. The anger and fear and loneliness just grow and grow. You're afraid of what you might do if—when—people return. You fear that in the end, the most dangerous spirit in Winchester Mystery House might just be you.

THE END

To follow another path, turn to page 12.
To learn more about the Winchester Mystery House,
turn to page 97.

You watch as Amir starts pulling bottles from the racks. He carefully looks at each label, keeping only the oldest vintages. With a shrug, you start doing the same. With almost a dozen bottles tucked under your arms, in your pants, and even under your chin, you emerge from the cellar, clunking and clanking with a noise that just might wake the dead.

Amir takes off down the hallway. You're trying to carry so many bottles that you can't even keep up. You're constantly stopping, shifting the bottles around, trying not to let any slip from your grasp. "Wait! Slow down, Amir!" you shout. But he's already around a corner.

That's when you feel the cold hand on your shoulder. You scream. Three bottles drop to the floor. The sound of shattering glass rings out.

You whirl around to see a white female shape. Her mouth is open, and her eyes are nothing more than deep black pits.

The rest of your bottles fall to the floor. The floor runs blood red with the priceless wine. The figure screams—a hollow, empty sound. As you turn to run, your shoes slip on the wine. You go over sideways, your head slamming into the wall.

It takes a moment before you completely lose consciousness. The last thing you see is a white blur, descending down upon you.

THE END

To follow another path, turn to page 12.
To learn more about The Winchester Mystery House, turn to page 97.

"Stop," you tell Amir. "This isn't ours. Look, we'll mark our way back." You pull some wadded up paper from your pocket and tear off a small piece, rolling it into a little ball. You drop it onto the floor. "See, like a trail of breadcrumbs. That way we can find this place again. But these bottles aren't ours to take."

Amir sighs. "Yeah, I guess you're right. Sorry. I just got excited there for a minute."

The two of you move back up the stairs and through the Hall of Fires. It's a frustrating trek through the house, but you make slow progress.

When you finally find your way out, you feel as though a weight has been lifted off your chest. Outside, two police cars sit, along with Amir's dad and your parents. "Thank goodness!" says Amir's dad. "I called the police when you two disappeared. We were terrified you'd get lost in that crazy house!"

the sewing room

You return to the house the next day, along with your parents, one of the property's owners, and one of the house's tour guides.

"So you're telling me that you just stumbled across a wine cellar that's been undiscovered for almost a century?" the owner asks. You can tell she doesn't really believe you. Following your trail of breadcrumbs, you weave deep inside the house, into a part that has been closed since the great earthquake of 1906.

Turn the page.

When you lead the group down the old stairs into the musty wine cellar, silence hangs over the room. After a few moments, the celebration begins. "You don't know what you've found here," the tour guide tells you. "These bottles are worth millions! And don't you worry. I'm sure the owners are going to give you a hefty finder's fee. You're going to be rich!"

You smile. But despite the noisy excitement of the discovery, you swear you can hear the distant pound-pound-pounding of a hammer in the distance.

THE END

To follow another path, turn to page 12.
To learn more about the Winchester Mystery House,
turn to page 97.

You need help, but you're not sure anyone is going to believe your story. There's no way you want to have to explain yourself to the authorities here.

You hurry down out of the bell tower and head for a deeper level. You'll find a nice quiet spot to hunker down and wait this out. As you bound down a small, curving staircase, your foot catches a step wrong. CRACK!

Some of the staircases were built with steps only 2 inches (5 centimeters) tall. They may have been built so Sarah Winchester, who had arthritis later in life, could climb the stairs more easily.

Turn the page.

Pain surges up your leg as you fall sprawling down. You slam your head hard on a wall and black out for a few moments.

As you come to, everything is blurry, as if a blanket of fog has descended upon the house. You try to stand, but your ankle won't tolerate any pressure. As pain and dizziness overcome you, you fall once again into a heap.

Some of the rooms in the Winchester Mystery House remain unfinished today.

You shout, hoping that someone—anyone—will come. But as the echoes of your pleas grow weaker and the pain in your ankle and head become unbearable, you start to lose hope. You're hurt and alone, deep in the world's most mysterious house. If only you'd signaled that police officer, they'd know to come looking. But now, you're going to need a miracle to make it out alive.

THE END

To follow another path, turn to page 12.
To learn more about the Winchester Mystery House, turn to page 97.

You don't know why a police car might be here, but one thing is certain. You're lost and in desperate need of help. You shout, you wave your arms, you try everything to get the officer's attention. But you're just too far away. The wind carries your shouts away before they can ever reach the car. And unless someone is looking directly at the bell tower, they're never going to see you.

For a moment, you feel helpless. Then you look up.

The bell. Of course! If you want to get attention, you've got the perfect tool right above you. You grab the cord and start to ring the bell furiously. It doesn't take long for someone to notice that. Within minutes, an officer speaking into a bullhorn tells you to stay put. "We're coming to get you. Your parents are on their way. They'll be here soon," he says.

Less than twenty minutes later, an officer is leading you outside, into the arms of your worried parents. "What about Amir?" you ask.

One of the most well-known statues on the property is Chief Little Fawn. It was rumored that Sarah Winchester built the statue to ward off spirits of Native Americans killed by Winchester rifles.

Turn the page.

"We're still looking," the officer answers. "We'll let you know as soon as we find him."

Minutes turn into hours. Hours into days. Days into weeks. But there's no sign of Amir. It's as if he simply vanished.

Amir's disappearance is a mystery. For a few days, the story gets intense news coverage. You decline all interviews. But after a week, most everyone has forgotten about your friend. You never do. It eats at you. You have nightmares. All you can feel is overwhelming guilt and shame.

Years later, you can no longer take it. You return to the house. As you enter the room where Sarah Winchester held her séances, you can't help but shudder. For a fleeting moment, you're all but certain Amir is standing right next to you. You have a powerful sense of being watched.

But it's not a dark feeling. Not scary at all. Instead, you feel a strange warmth. You feel … forgiveness. The emotion is so strong that you have to drop to your knees and close your eyes.

But just as quickly as that presence appeared, it is gone. Suddenly, it's just a room. Empty. Your friend is gone, a devastating reminder of your night spent in the Winchester Mystery House. But now, finally, you feel ready to move on with your life.

THE END

To follow another path, turn to page 12.
To learn more about The Winchester Mystery House, turn to page 97.

"Leave now!" shouts the spirit possessing Amir's body. "Leave! Leave! Leave!"

You gather every shred of courage in your body and lunge for Amir's arm. His face darkens. A cold blast of wind rips through the room. The floor and walls seem to tremble.

The doors fly open with a loud bang. Outside, shadows flicker through the halls.

Amir, or whoever he is, charges out into the hallway. He screams again, then bolts down the hall. You back up against the wall in terror as the strange, dancing shadows whisk away in his wake.

"Ruuuuuuuun!" shouts whatever it is that has a hold on your friend.

Your heart won't stop racing. Sarah Winchester was right. This place is overrun with angry spirits. There's nothing you can do for Amir. You have to get out.

You waste no time. You charge through the halls, searching for an exit. In the distance, deep inside the house, you hear strange wails. Screams. Crashes. At every turn, you veer away from the sounds, until finally, you come upon an unlocked window. You dive outside into some shrubs. You run out into the parking lot, never turning back.

You won't stop running until you find help. You just hope it's not too late for your friend.

THE END

To follow another path, turn to page 12.
To learn more about the Winchester Mystery House,
turn to page 97.

"Let go of him!" you plead. "We'll go. We'll leave right now. But you have to let go of my friend."

The face, which is Amir's—but isn't—regards you coldly, as if deciding. Then, with something that looks like resignation, the spirit speaks to you one last time. "Run. Don't stop."

the Stairwell to Nowhere

A blast of cold air rushes past you. At the same moment, the doors fly open. Amir slumps to the floor. For a moment, he's unconscious. But slowly, he comes back.

"Is it you?" you ask your friend. "Amir, is it you?"

He shakes his head in confusion. "What are you talking about?"

Thank goodness! He doesn't remember any of it!

You grab Amir's arm and help him to his feet. "We have to go now. Come on!"

Amir rubs his head. "Huh? What's going on? Why the sudden ..."

"Just trust me," you interrupt. "I'll explain everything later. Right now, we have to go."

Turn the page.

The hallways have turned ice cold. At the end of the hall, a dim blue light floats before a closed door. Strange, dancing shadows seem to gather all around it, as if it's drawing them like a magnet. You don't wait to see more.

You twist and turn through the house, stumbling over staircases with steps far too small, running into dead ends, and finally emerging through the same doors you entered, out into the garden. You don't stop running until Winchester Mystery House is far, far behind you. One thing is certain. You won't ever be going back there again.

THE END

To follow another path, turn to page 12.
To learn more about the Winchester Mystery House,
turn to page 97.

People have reported the smell of soup in the Winchester Mystery House kitchens.

Chicken soup? That makes no sense. The house is empty. In fact, you seem to remember reading that the kitchens in the Winchester house weren't even in operation anymore. Yet there's no doubt about what you smell. As your stomach growls once again, you resolve to find out.

Turn the page.

You descend down a long, narrow staircase
before coming to a hallway lined with mirrors.
As you pass the final mirror, you catch something
out of the corner of your vision. You whirl,
heart racing. There, in the mirror, just over your
shoulder. A face. It's there for just an instant. With
a blink, it's gone.

Breathing rapidly, you whirl back and forth,
searching the hallway. Empty. There's no one here.
Yet … the face. You could have sworn it was there.

You shake your head and ball your fists,
desperately trying to gather your wits. "Nothing
supernatural," you tell yourself. "Just my
imagination running wild." You almost believe it.
Your breathing slows. The thumping in your chest
quiets, just a little. Somewhat composed, you
enter a large, empty kitchen area. Suddenly, the
smell of chicken soup is gone.

SLAM! The noise of the door crashing shut makes you jump. The room falls into darkness. You rush to the door, fighting to open it, but it won't budge. You scream and shout, but the sounds only seem to echo back at you.

You're trapped. Deep inside this crazy house, all alone. Amir won't ever find you here. You can only hold out some small hope that someone else will. But as you slump down to the cold floor, you hear a deep, resonating sound that fills you with dread.

It's laughter.

THE END

To follow another path, turn to page 12.
To learn more about the Winchester Mystery House, turn to page 97.

One room contains panels of glass surrounded by a railing so you can see into the servants' kitchen below.

You try to follow the sound. But every turn seems to direct you away from it. When you go up a staircase, the sound seems to come from below. When you double back and go back down, the thumping seems to come from overhead.

And with every step you take, a feeling of dread grows. You can't shake the sensation of being watched. You sense movement at the edges of your vision, but as you whirl about, there's never anything there. You hear whispers, but they're so soft you can't make out what's being said. You can't even be sure you're not imagining them.

As you ascend a staircase, shouting Amir's name, something appears in front of you. It's the shape of a man, dressed in overalls. The ghost is dressed in clothes from the early part of the 1900s, perhaps as the laborers who built this house might have dressed. For a moment, the spirit just stands there. Uncertain what to do, you reach out toward it. The ghost opens its mouth, wider … wider … wider. It screams. The sound is unlike anything you've ever heard. It's more a rattle than a shriek.

Turn the page.

You step back, stumbling in your panic. You look up in horror as the ghost lifts a hammer and swings down on you. Your screams echo through the hallways. You feel your fragile tie to reality—to your own sanity—finally snap.

They find you two days later, wandering aimlessly through an abandoned part of the house. An ambulance rushes you to the hospital. No one ever finds Amir. But in truth, he's not the only one left behind in the labyrinth of Winchester Mystery House. Your body may have escaped, but your mind never did. It remains behind, caught in a nightmare from which you can never escape.

THE END

To follow another path, turn to page 12.
To learn more about the Winchester Mystery House,
turn to page 97.

That's not Amir. There's a deadness in his eyes. They stare at you, almost through you, as if hungry.

You turn and slam into one of the doors. Then another, and another, until your shoulders ache. None of them budge. In desperation, you fling open the only door left in this room, a closet. Only this is no closet. It's a secret passage!

a door in the Winchester Mystery House that opens to a solid wall

Turn the page.

You dive inside, flinging the door shut behind you. As you cross the threshold, you catch your foot. You topple over at a bad angle, slamming your head into the floor. You're knocked almost senseless by the blow.

Pain surges through your entire body. On your hands and knees, you stagger back, just waiting for the door to open, for whatever has possessed your friend's body to come through. But it doesn't.

For a moment, the only sound is the thumping of your own heart. Then, moments later, footsteps. The sound of a door creaking open. Finally, the sound of that same door slamming shut.

"Amir?" you call out softly, almost afraid to make a sound. No reply.

You try to stand. But dizziness instantly overcomes you. You fall back to the floor in a heap, only half conscious. Desperate, you reach for the door. But there's no handle on this side. You're trapped! And your strength is rapidly fading.

Again, you try to shout out to your friend, but your voice is weak. Your fingers scratch at the trap door, but can't find any grip. The darkness is creeping in around the edges of your vision. You lay your head down. You'll just sleep for a few minutes. Just a few minutes … a few minutes.

It's a long, long sleep. One that you never wake from. The Winchester Mystery House has one more spirit to haunt its endless halls.

THE END

To follow another path, turn to page 12.
To learn more about the Winchester Mystery House,
turn to page 97.

Amir is right. There's a ghost in the corner of the room talking to you. Why are you still here?

You turn to run. Amir is already out the door. But before you can leave, a massive gust of cold wind slams the door shut. BOOM! The whole room seems to shake. You can hear Amir trying to open the door from the other side, screaming through it, throwing his body into it. But the door won't budge.

Visitors have reported seeing chandeliers swaying without reason at the Winchester Mystery House.

A vase falls from a small table, smashing onto the floor and shattering into a thousand pieces. From above, a long, low creaking sound fills the room. The chandelier! You dive into a corner just seconds before it slams down onto the floor. Candle wax and flames spill out. The flames spread quickly across the room's old rugs. Within seconds the room is like a blazing furnace. One wall is engulfed in flames, then another.

Finally, the door flies open. Amir stares inside, horrified. The flames are spreading at frightening speed.

"Run!" yells Amir. You don't need convincing.

Smoke pours out into the hallway as you duck through the doorway. You and Amir move as fast as you can, your only goal to run away from the flames. It seems like hours before you come to a window.

Turn the page.

Amir throws a chair through and lowers himself down. You're right behind. The two of you sprint from the house. Breathless, you finally stop to turn around. Thick gray smoke rises from above the house. You can see fingers of flame over parts of the roof. Soon, the wailing of fire engines fills the air.

When it's all over, when the flames are finally out, the house is no longer standing. And no one believes your story.

"There are no open flames in there. Someone would have had to light one," says the police officer taking your statement. He looks at you with a scowl. "Arson is a serious charge. I sure hope you've got a better story to tell the judge."

THE END

To follow another path, turn to page 12.
To learn more about the Winchester Mystery House,
turn to page 97.

Twelve candles lit, one unlit. Suddenly, you remember reading a story about Sarah Winchester before you came to work at the Mystery House. She was obsessed with the number 13. She built the number into every facet of the house. Could this be her spirit, restless over the unlit 13th candle?

It's crazy. But you feel compelled to help. Warily, you remove a vase from a small table, trying not to take your gaze off the ghost for more than a moment. The idea that she's there, watching you, lurking, makes your skin crawl. But you feel like you have to do this. You move the table under the chandelier and step up. You can just barely reach, but you're able to remove the unlit candle, dip its wick into the flame of another, and replace it.

Turn the page.

As you step down from the table, you look to the corner. There's nothing there. The room seems brighter, and not just because of the thirteenth candle. The sinister feeling is gone too. It's almost like a weight has been lifted—not just from your shoulders, but from the house itself.

The Winchester Mystery House features many windows that gaze into other rooms of the house.

Amir steps into the room timidly.

"She's gone?"

You take one last glance. You know that Sarah Winchester was a frightened, deeply superstitious woman. Is there any reason to believe her spirit wouldn't be the same? Whatever the reason, you feel like you've helped ease her suffering in some small way.

You turn to your friend. "Yeah, she's gone. Now let's find our way out of this place."

THE END

To follow another path, turn to page 12.
To learn more about the Winchester Mystery House,
turn to page 97.

That's it. You're done. An adventure in one of the world's strangest homes sounded like a lot of fun when you first came here. An hour ago, you couldn't have resisted the opportunity to explore a mystery such as this one.

The switchback staircase features 44 steps but only goes up about 9 feet (2.7 meters).

But not anymore. Ghostly historical flashbacks, cryptic messages etched in the floor, and an inviting open door? No thanks. Your days of seeking adventure are over.

"Let's get out of here," you tell Amir.

"You don't have to ask me twice. This place is nuts."

Of course, getting out is easier said than done ...

THE END

To follow another path, turn to page 12.
To learn more about the Winchester Mystery House,
turn to page 97.

You close your eyes. Thump! Thump! You're done with this wild goose chase. Even if you try to follow that sound, you'll just get yourself more lost. There's only one thing to do—get out and trust Amir to do the same.

Heart racing and hands shaking, you creep down the dimly lit corridors. Behind you, a floorboard creaks. You don't even turn around. As you pass though some sort of study with walls lined with ancient volumes, you feel a sudden chill. Whispers. Soft, more like shuffling papers than a human voice. You can make out only a single, sharp syllable—"Mine!"

You break into a run, charging through the house, twisting and turning almost at random. The sense of being watched is overpowering. As you round a corner, your foot slips on an old rug. You slam straight into another figure.

You scream as you sprawl to the floor. The figure lets out a blood-curdling shriek. It's almost on top of you!

As you try to scramble to your feet, you get a better look. Your heart nearly leaps out of your chest. This is no ghost!

"Amir! Amir! It's me!" you call, your voice cracking.

The shrieking stops. You drop down to a knee and grab your friend, wrapping him up in a desperate hug. You're both gasping for breath. But in that moment, reunited, it all seems impossibly absurd. All the emotion—the fear, the dread, the relief—pours out, at first in tears, but soon in rolling laughter. Despite everything that has happened, you feel confident again.

Turn the page.

A corner room provides a beautiful view of the pristine gardens below.

"Let's get out of here," Amir says as you both pull yourselves to your feet. "And this time, we stick together, no matter what."

Years later, your memory of that night is faded. You recall only fragmented bits and pieces of your adventure. You remember little of how you and Amir finally let yourselves out through a third-story window. But what you'll never forget, what remains as clear in your mind as the moment it happened, is that feeling of finding your friend again. Of all that you faced in Winchester Mystery House that night, that is the one moment that endures.

THE END

To follow another path, turn to page 12.
To learn more about the Winchester Mystery House,
turn to page 97.

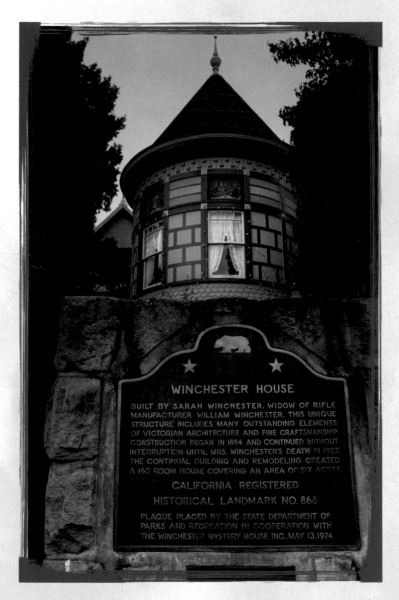

The Winchester Mystery House is a registered
California landmark.

A Dark History of the Winchester Mystery House

The story in this book is a blend of fact and fiction. It's supposed to be fun. But the true story of Winchester Mystery House is a tale of tragedy, loneliness, and desperation. The home stands as a symbol of one woman's life and loss.

Sarah Lockwood Pardee was born around 1840. She was a bright, well-educated young woman. In 1862 she married William Wirt Winchester, heir to the fortune of the Winchester Repeating Arms Company. The company manufactured the hugely popular Winchester rifle. Four years later, Sarah gave birth to a daughter, Annie. The future looked bright for Sarah and her young family. But her life soon took a dark turn.

the Winchester family tree

Baby Annie grew sick with a disease called marasmus. She lived only a few weeks. Sarah was devastated. She fell into a deep depression. Then in 1881, William died. Sarah became convinced that her family was haunted. She thought the spirits of the people killed by Winchester rifles were out for revenge.

She also believed that the spirit of her dead husband had spoken to her. He told her to move west and build a new home. To confuse the angry spirits, she should never stop building it.

In 1884 Winchester bought land and an unfinished barn in California's Santa Clara Valley. The construction of the mansion started almost immediately. Winchester used her great fortune from the rifle company to hire builders on a nearly constant basis.

Carpenters worked day and night. The house was built room by room, with no real master plan. Winchester believed that a nonsensical design would keep evil spirits at bay.

The house started with eight rooms. By 1900 it had sprawled out to a towering seven stories.

Winchester was a mystery herself. She invited children to play in her lavish gardens, yet she was also very secretive. She hid her face behind a veil at all times. Some say she would even fire any workers who accidentally saw her face.

a view outside from the Door to Nowhere

Neighbors reported the sound of bells at 2 a.m. within the house. Winchester believed that was the time spirits could come and go from their world to this one. She also had a fascination with the number 13. The number appears throughout the house. When she received a chandelier containing 12 candles, she ordered that one more be added to make 13.

Much of Winchester's energy was spent keeping evil spirits away. Some say she never slept in the same room two nights in a row. And yet Winchester welcomed friendly spirits. She supposedly devoted an entire room—her famous Blue Room—to communicating with the dead.

A 1906 earthquake damaged the house. But it didn't stop Winchester. Repairs were carried out right alongside new construction. Nothing would stop her from building, and building ... and building.

Late in life, Winchester suffered from arthritis. She had workers build staircases with very short steps to make climbing easier. She was always cold, so she had them build dozens of fireplaces. One room, the Hall of Fires, contains four fireplaces, as well as several vents leading to a coal furnace.

Winchester died in her sleep in 1922. At the time, the house contained at least 160 rooms, miles of hallways, 47 fireplaces, and about 2,000 doors. According to reports, upon hearing of her death, builders left the job on the spot, even leaving nails half-pounded.

The house was sold and opened for tours. The illusionist Harry Houdini visited the house in 1924. Some sources say Houdini gave the house its nickname, Mystery House. The name stuck.

Since then, the Winchester Mystery House has been a tourist attraction. Many believe that the house remains a mystery. Some think it's possible that even today—after nearly a century—secret passageways and rooms may lie hidden deep within its walls, undiscovered after all this time.

Is the house haunted? Was Sarah Winchester right about spirits out for revenge? And if so, do their tormented souls lurk there still? What is the true mystery behind the Mystery House? Is it restless spirits? Or is it just the depths of grief and desperation felt by a mother and wife who lost her family?

FAST FACTS ABOUT WINCHESTER MYSTERY HOUSE

Location: San Jose, California

Style: Victorian

Construction started: 1884

Construction concluded: 1922

Rooms: 160 or more

Doors: 2,000 or more

Windows: 10,000 or more

Stairways: at least 47

Bathrooms: 13

Owner: Winchester Investments, LLC

TIMELINE

1840—Sarah Winchester is born Sarah Lockwood Pardee in New Haven, Connecticut.

1860—The Henry Repeating Rifle is developed for the Winchester Repeating Arms Company.

1861–1865—The Civil War takes place.

September 30, 1862—Sarah marries William Wirt Winchester.

July 24, 1866—The Winchesters' daughter, Annie, dies from a mysterious disease.

1873—The Winchester Repeating Rifle model known as the "gun that won the West" is developed.

March 7, 1881—William Winchester dies from tuberculosis.

1884—Sarah moves from Connecticut to San Jose, California; construction on the Winchester House begins.

1906—A huge earthquake hits San Francisco, severely damaging the house.

1911—*The New York Times* publishes an article stating that Sarah Winchester is "lying at the point of death"—even though she doesn't die for another 11 years.

1914–1918—World War I takes place.

September 5, 1922—Sarah Winchester dies in her sleep; construction on the house stops.

1923—The house is opened to the public for the first time.

1973—Renovation on the Winchester Mystery House begins.

1974—The house is named a California Registered Historic Landmark and is added to the National Register of Historic Places.

GLOSSARY

adrenaline (uh-DREH-nuh-luhn)—a chemical the body produces when a person is excited

apparition (ap-uh-RISH-uhn)—the visible appearance of a ghost

arthritis (ar-THRY-tuhs)—a disease that makes people's bone joints swollen and painful

chandelier (SHAN-duh-LEER)—a hanging light with branches for light bulbs or candles

cold spot (COLD SPOT)—an area of intense cold that cannot be explained by natural causes; cold spots are said to be a sign of a ghostly presence

corridor (KOR-uh-dohr)—a long passageway

cryptic (KRIP-tik)—mysterious or having an obscure meaning

engulf (in-GULF)—to sweep over something to surround or cover it completely

flashback (FLASH-back)—scene that returns to earlier events

heir (AIR)—someone who has been or will be left a title, property, or money

illusionist (i-LOO-zhuhn-ist)—someone who performs tricks that appear to be real but aren't

ornate (or-NAYT)—elaborately or excessively decorated

paranormal (pair-uh-NOR-muhl)—having to do with an unexplained event that has no scientific explanation

repeating rifle (ruh-PEE-ting RI-ful)—a single-barreled rifle that contains multiple rounds of ammunition

séance (SAY-ahns)—a meeting to contact the spirits of the dead

sinister (SIN-uh-stuhr)—something harmful or evil

supernatural (soo-pur-NACH-ur-uhl)—something that cannot be given an ordinary explanation

vintage (VIN-tij)—from the past

OTHER PATHS TO EXPLORE

In this book you've seen how terrifying being alone in a haunted space can be. But haunted places can mean different things to different people. Seeing an experience from many points of view is an important part of understanding it.

Here are a few ideas for other haunted points of view to explore:

+ What do you think daily life was like for Sarah Winchester? Would it have been easy to live such an odd, secretive life? What would her fear of ghosts have been like?

+ Imagine you have been hired to help build the Winchester House. One day you are asked to build a twisted hallway, the next day a set of tiny steps leading nowhere. Would you be frightened to keep working, or interested in what other projects you might work on?

+ Many visitors to the Winchester Mystery House have reported seeing ghosts and hearing other paranormal activity. Would you take a haunted tour to seek out the spirits that may still live in the house? What do you think you could expect to see?

READ MORE

Chandler, Matt. *Bachelor's Grove Cemetery and Other Haunted Places of the Midwest.* North Mankato, Minn.: Capstone Press, 2014.

Henneberg, Susan. *Investigating Ghosts and the Spirit World.* New York: Britannica Educational Publishing in Association with Rosen Educational Services, 2015.

Shea, Therese. *Haunted!: The Queen Mary.* New York: Gareth Stevens Publishing, 2013.

INTERNET SITES

Use FactHound to find Internet sites related to this book. All of the sites on FactHound have been researched by our staff.

Here's all you do:
Visit *www.facthound.com*
Type in this code: 9781515725770

INDEX